Rain Forests
of the
World

Volume 1
Africa–Bioluminescence

MARSHALL CAVENDISH
NEW YORK • LONDON • TORONTO • SYDNEY

Marshall Cavendish
99 White Plains Road
Tarrytown, New York
10591-9001

Website: www.marshallcavendish.com

Consulting Editors: Rolf E. Johnson, Nathan E. Kraucunas

Contributing Authors: Theresa Greenaway, Jill Bailey, Michael Chinery, Malcolm Penny, Mike Linley, Philip Steele, Chris Oxlade, Ken Preston-Mafham, Rod Preston-Mafham, Clare Oliver, Don Birchfield

Discovery Books
    Managing Editor: Paul Humphrey
    Project Editor: Gianna Williams
    Text Editor: Valerie Weber
    Designer: Ian Winton
    Cartographer: Stefan Chabluk
    Illustrators: Jim Channell, Stuart Lafford, Christian Webb

Marshall Cavendish
    Editor: Marian Armstrong
    Editorial Director: Paul Bernabeo

(Frontispiece) Heliconia Rendulata (cover) waterfall, Southern Highlands Province, Papua New Guinea

Editor's Note: Many systems of dating have been used by different cultures throughout history. *Rain Forests of the World* uses B.C.E. (Before Common Era) and C.E. (Common Era) instead of B.C. (Before Christ) and A.D. (Anno Domini, "In the Year of Our Lord") out of respect for the diversity of the world's peoples.

The publishers would like to thank the following for their permission to reproduce photographs:
2 Fritz Polking/Frank Lane Picture Agency, 3 Giacomo Pirozzi/Panos Pictures, 4 Stephen Dalton/Natural History Photographic Agency, 5 Joe McDonald/Bruce Coleman Limited, 6 Luiz Claudio Marigo/Bruce Coleman Collection, 7 Ken Preston-Mafham/ Premaphotos Wildlife, 8 Michael Fogden/Oxford Scientific Films, 9 M. P. L. Fogden/Bruce Coleman Collection, 10 Ken Preston-Mafham/Premaphotos Wildlife, 11 Eric Soder/NHPA, 13 Michael Fogden/Oxford Scientific Films, 14 Gerard Lacz/FLPA, 16 Werner Layer/Bruce Coleman Collection, 17 Clive Bromhall/Oxford Scientific Films, 18 Jurgen & Christine Sohns/FLPA, 19 Jim Clare/Partridge Films Ltd./Oxford Scientific Films, 20 & 21 Martin Adler/Panos Pictures, 23 Harold Taylor/Oxford Scientific Films, 24 Chris Mattison/FLPA, 25 Mandal Ranjit/FLPA, 26 Paul Franklin/Oxford Scientific Films, 27 Ken Preston-Mafham/Premaphotos Wildlife, 28 Dr. Jeremy Burgess/Science Photo Library, 29 Alain Compost/Bruce Coleman Collection, 30 Stephen Dalton/NHPA, 31 Mary Plage/Bruce Coleman Collection, 32 ANT/NHPA, 33 Jurgen & Christine Sohns/FLPA, 34, 35, 36, 37 & 38 Ken Preston-Mafham/Premaphotos Wildlife, Pavel German/NHPA, 40 Martin Harvey/NHPA, 41 Ken Preston-Mafham/Premaphotos Wildlife, 44 ANT/NHPA, 45 Haroldo Palo Jr./NHPA, 46 Jorge Sierra/Oxford Scientific Films, 47 Michael Fogden/Oxford Scientific Films

Library of Congress Cataloging-in-Publication Data
Rain forests of the world.
          p. cm.
      Includes bibliographical references and index.
      Contents: v. 1. Africa-bioluminescence — v. 2. Biomass-clear-cutting — v. 3. Climate and weather-emergent — v. 4. Endangered species-food web — v. 5. Forest fire-iguana — v. 6. Indonesia-manatee — v. 7. Mangrove forest-orangutan — v. 8. Orchid-red panda — v. 9. Reforestation-spider — v. 10. Squirrel-Yanomami people — v. 11. Index.
        ISBN 0-7614-7254-1 (set)
        1. Rain forests—Encyclopedias.   I. Marshall Cavendish Corporation.
    QH86 .R39 2002
    578.734—dc21
                                                    2001028460

ISBN 0-7614-7254-1 (set)
ISBN 0-7614-7255-X (vol. 1)

Printed and bound in Italy

07 06 05 04 03 02   6 5 4 3 2 1

Contents of the Set

Volume 8

Volume 9

Volume 10

Volume 11

Contents by Category

Rain Forest Types and Characteristics

Peoples of the Rain Forest

Animals

Plants, Algae, and Microorganisms

General Topics

Rain forests are among the most complex, rich, and valuable ecosystems found on our planet. They are also among the most endangered by human activity. From Borneo to Brazil, Congo to Tongass, the rain forests of our planet are rapidly disappearing at the hands of humans. Those same hands also hold the key to preserving the rain forests. By systematically studying the rain forest and learning from the indigenous peoples who still live there, we have discovered profound links that intimately connect the human species with the forest and with the other life-forms on our planet.

In the last thirty years—a period of intense scientific activity—we have learned a great deal about these critical biomes and the amazing plants, animals, and microorganisms that live within them. We have begun to understand the rain forest's wealth of biological diversity, or biodiversity. When we use the term *biodiversity*, we are referring to more than just a simple list of plants and animals living in a particular place on our planet, a coral reef for example. Biodiversity is also an exploration of interconnections—the variety of genetic materials within each individual species, the variety of species, and most important, the variety of ecosystems and landscapes within which species evolve and coexist. This is biodiversity. This is the evolving tree of life.

Rain forests are full of life: life that has evolved over millions of years and in relatively stable, warm, and wet environments. Some scientists estimate between 30 and 100 million interrelated species exist on our planet today. Many of these are found in the rain forest. The forest is also a place of connections, of pieces to the biodiversity puzzle. In the rain forest we find complex interrelationships between living things, unique adaptations to survival in different environments, complex animal behaviors in social organisms, and other amazing evolutionary specializations within and between species. Nowhere on Earth are these relationships more plentiful than in the places we call rain forests. We are discovering how individual species function in communities containing many species, how communities function within ecosystems, and how ecosystems function within biomes and, finally, the biosphere.

Tropical rain forests are scattered in an uneven green belt between the Tropic of Cancer, north of the equator, and the Tropic of Capricorn, south of it. They grow in regions of relatively low elevation, where heat, humidity, and frequent rainfall nurture a diversity of life-forms. Rain forests are truly amazing places. Often referred to as "jungles," these emerald forests are beautiful and inspiring, with their enormous, towering broad-leaved evergreen trees and countless plant and animal forms, from hundreds of parasitic worms to herds of elephants. Only recently have rain forests slowly begun revealing the secrets of interconnected life-forms that have evolved over millions of years into millions of species.

Rain forests are not only home to plants, animals, and microorganisms—they are home to people as well. Indigenous groups from the Amazon to the Congo, Papua New Guinea to British Columbia continue to live as they have for generations. The depth of knowledge these peoples have is only now being comprehended by Western society. The wisdom of shamans, and their knowledge of forest organisms, should not be lost. Opening remote forests to exploitation leads to a clash of cultures, as indigenous peoples have first contact with modern culture. These native peoples, with their intimate and unique understanding of rain forest plants and animals, are struggling to maintain their way of life.

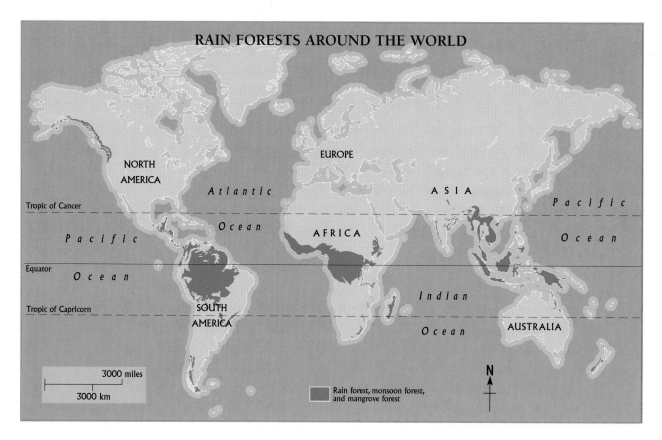

RAIN FORESTS AROUND THE WORLD

The lowland evergreen tropical rain forests—the richest, most biologically diverse communities of living things on Earth—are also great, natural laboratories. Here, women and men from around the world are carefully studying the structure, genetic makeup, composition, and ecology of these critically important biomes: from the simplest fungus to the complex social structure exhibited by one million army ants moving over the forest floor. Millions upon millions of other plants, animals, and microorganisms are still largely unknown. New species are named every day.

One of the most important new areas of research is "bio-prospecting," the search for specimens that might possess chemical keys to treating major human diseases, such as cancer or AIDS. A growing number of scientific researchers—and most important, the indigenous peoples of the forest—are finding incredible new uses for ethnobotanical knowledge and biodiversity. It is estimated that between 30 and 50 percent of the pharmaceuticals being used today come directly from, or are derived from, enzymes and other chemicals found in rain forest plants, animals, and microbial life. Each species of the millions of rain forest organisms has made its unique adaptation to survive the challenges of life, and the information encoded in its genes may have an immense value for humanity.

Not all rain forests are tropical. Some grow in temperate zones. Most of these temperate rain forests occur along coastal areas, swept with rain and often shrouded with mists. These green, ancient biomes have their own unique ecology. One such temperate rain forest is the Tongass National Forest, located along the western coast of Alaska. This is a vast, quiet world where the effects of human activity are felt heavily amid the biologically rich old-growth habitat that is being rapidly cut and fragmented. The forests that grow on the northwest coast of North America and those in the island chains of the South Pacific all grow in temperate zones. Coastal conifers and great ferns are two of the prominent plant forms of the temperate rain forests.

Time is running out for the plants and animals of the rain forest. About half of the world's original equatorial rain forest is already gone. Once unbroken belts of green, these forests are being clear-cut, strip-mined, drowned by hydroelectric projects, bulldozed, polluted, and burned. Most development schemes have not harvested these forests in a sustainable manner. Rain forests are being exploited and destroyed at a rate so rapid that many scientists estimate that by the middle of the 21st century, the vast majority of rain forests—along with the organisms that live there—will have completely vanished. No one really knows what this will mean to the human species, but the environmental changes being predicted, such as higher global temperatures and an increase in the severity of seasonal storms, may endanger our own human survival.

However, thanks to a better understanding of rain forest ecosystems and the important role they play in the functioning of the planet's biosphere and climate, conservation efforts are well underway.

Countries such as Costa Rica in Central America are leading the way in the study and conservation of their forests. Over 27 percent of Costa Rican land is now protected and devoted to the preservation of biological diversity. In some wildlife reserves, a careful extraction of resources for scientific research, biological inventories, and environmental education is permitted.

Awareness has grown in recent years of the threats to the world's rain forests and the importance of trying to preserve as much forest as possible. Many conservationists, scientists, celebrities, indigenous groups, governments, and other concerned citizens have been at the forefront in alerting the world to the incalculable consequences of their destruction.

The future of our planet's rain forests is anything but certain. The needs of ever-growing human populations, along with the political and social pressures caused by the unequal distribution of wealth, are complex issues that continue to impact nature. We will be grappling with these issues well into the middle of this century.

It is a challenge to compile any list of the biggest rain forests, or the most diverse, most unknown, or most endangered. All rain forests are unique, yet all have much in common. In order to understand the whole, we must first understand the parts.

The scientific and technical team that assembled *Rain Forests of the World* has produced a reference set that provides some of the most recent information in a rapidly changing field of research. It is difficult to appreciate and preserve what we don't understand, and science is one critically important way to understand nature. Created with the goal of providing a useful reference for rain forest information and biodiversity issues, *Rain Forests of the World* has endeavored to provide accurate, scientific information integrated with issues of cultural diversity.

There is still hope for preserving what remains of Earth's precious biological diversity, and that hope lies in human hands. There is still so much to learn. We are all beginning to understand, through scientific study, exploration, and the knowledge of indigenous peoples, the places we call rain forests.

For all their majestic beauty, they are very fragile.

Rolf E. Johnson
Milwaukee Public Museum
February 2001

Rain Forests of the World takes an encyclopedic view of rain forests, their plants, animals, and peoples, as well as issues affecting rain forests, such as deforestation and the efforts being made worldwide to protect them from further destruction.

Volume One contains an introduction by the consultant for the set, Rolf E. Johnson, Director of the Center for Media and Instructional Technology and Associate Curator of Paleontology at the Milwaukee Public Museum. Johnson, an Emmy Award–winning producer of science and natural history programs, is currently working on tropical forest restoration and conservation projects in Costa Rica and Nicaragua. He has authored over 65 scientific and technical publications on conservation, biology, education, and paleontology. In his introduction, Rolf Johnson explains graphically why rain forests are such fascinating places, and why it is so important to try to understand and preserve them.

Entries in the set are arranged alphabetically. They have been divided into five color-coded categories for easy reference. The color-coding of each entry indicates which category it belongs to:

- **Rain Forest Types and Characteristics**
- **Rain Forest Peoples**
- **Animals**
- **Plants, Algae, and Microorganisms**
- **General Topics**

Any entry longer than one page starts with a **Key Facts** box highlighting special points of interest regarding the topic. Geographically defined subjects are illustrated with a map.

The entries are lavishly illustrated with full-color photographs, accompanied by detailed captions that enhance the text.

Many entries feature **In Focus** boxes with more detailed information on a fascinating aspect of the topic being discussed.

Many difficult, unfamiliar, or foreign words are followed by a simple pronunciation guide.

Every entry ends with a **Check these out** list of color-coded headings that the reader can refer to for more information within the set.

At the end of each volume is a **Glossary** with concise definitions of difficult words mentioned in the text and an **Index**.

Volume 11, which contains the comprehensive index to the set, will help you find references to particular subjects. There is a general index, as well as indexes on the following specific topics:

- Birds
- Invertebrates
- Mammals

- Peoples
- Places
- Plants, Algae, and Microorganisms
- Reptiles and Amphibians
- Research and Conservation
- Scientific Names

Volume 11 also includes the full **Glossary** for the set as well as a comprehensive **Further Reading** list.

Color-coded sidebars help the reader quickly find those articles that might be of interest in a specific category.

Longer articles have a **Key Facts** *box, which gives the reader a small preview of the subject matters being discussed and highlights some extraordinary facts.*

Longer articles feature one or more **In Focus** *boxes, which highlight an interesting facet of the article and explore it in more detail.*

Amazonia

Just slightly smaller than Australia, Amazonia is the vast region drained by the Amazon River. The Amazon is by far the world's largest river, only slightly shorter than the Nile in Africa but carrying much more water because of its enormous width. Some of the Amazon's 15,000 tributaries are themselves among the world's largest rivers. Even as far from the sea as Iquitos, Peru, nearly 2,000 miles (3,200 km) inland, the Amazon is still some 4 miles (6.5 km) wide, while in parts of Brazil it reaches the fantastic width of 40 miles (64 km). One-fifth of all the fresh water on Earth is contained within the Amazonian system.

Amazonian Rain Forest
Dense lowland tropical rain forest covers much of Amazonia, the largest area of such forest still

KEY FACTS

- The source of the Amazon River lies high in the Peruvian Andes at 16,950 ft. (5,168 m).

- Amazonia is home to more than 2,000 species of birds—almost a quarter of the world's total.

- Some of the Amazon's 15,000 tributaries are themselves among the world's largest rivers.

Flooded igapo forest along the Ariau River near the city of Manaus in Amazonia. The Ariau is a black-water river, stained dark brown by humus.

remaining anywhere and about half the current world total of rain forest.

Three main types of forest grow in Amazonia. Massive floods along the Amazon every year dictate where each forest lies. Areas that lie above the normal maximum flood level are called *tierra firme* forest,

meaning "hard ground." This type of forest holds the highest number of plant and animal species.

There are two types of seasonal flooded forest. The *varzea* is found along so-called white-water rivers, which carry huge amounts of silt eroded from high in the Andes Mountains. When the floods recede, this silt is left behind in the forest, acting as natural fertilizer and supporting an enormous range of plants and animals.

The second type of seasonal flooded forest, the *igapo* forest, is found along so-called black-water rivers, which are acidic and stained dark brown or black by humus. This type of forest supports less plant and animal life than the other two kinds of forest.

Amazonian Biodiversity
Amazonia probably harbors the world's highest diversity of fauna (animals) and flora (plants). Some 50,000 species of woody plants have already been described, around one-fifth of all those known on Earth. One area of Ecuadorian Amazonia boasts the world's richest variety of trees, with over 100 species per acre (250 per ha). The number of animal species probably runs into the millions, most of which are insects. In one small area of Rondônia, scientists have recorded over 1,800 species of butterflies, while more than 80 species of amphibians are known from another small area. Amazonia is the world's primate capital: it is home to around 45 species of primates, compared with just 30 for all of Africa. Some are still to be discovered.

Damage and Protection
Humans are destroying much of the original forest in Amazonia at an

increasing rate for farming, mining, and generating electricity.

Many plants and animals live only in Amazonia. Several of these species are endangered, but very little of the Amazonian area is currently protected in national parks or reserves.

IN FOCUS

A Sarayacu's Song
Amazonia has the world's highest diversity of amphibians. The Sarayacu tree frog is one of the most colorful in the region. It breeds in ponds in both untouched and secondary rain forest within a large area of the Amazonian region. It spends the day hunched down against a leaf, and becomes active at night. The male, which at around 1 in. (28 mm) long is smaller than the female, has a yellow vocal sac. He inflates it like bubblegum when he is calling, which he does from low vegetation in and around the edges of ponds.

Check these out:
- Amphibian ● Biodiversity ● Clear-Cutting
- Deforestation ● Endangered Species
- Fish ● Flooding ● Hydroelectricity
- Marmoset and Tamarin ● Primate
- Rain Forest ● River ● South America

6   7

Clear, concise maps are included in articles about rain forest countries, as well as in articles about peoples or animals that are located in a specific geographical area.

The **Check these out** *at the end of each article lists related articles in the encyclopedia for readers who would like more information, with a color-coded bullet point to help identify the categories each article belongs to.*

Contents of Volume 1

Africa is the world's second largest continent. Three-quarters of it lies within the Tropics, the warm regions on either side of the equator. These equatorial lands are the wettest in Africa.

At the very heart of the continent, the second largest rain forest zone in the world—after the Amazonian rain forest in South America—covers most of equatorial Africa. The rain forest zone includes both lowland and mountain regions. The mountain forests are often called cloud forests because they receive most of their moisture from the clouds that blanket their slopes rather than from rainfall.

Africa's Rain Forests

The largest area of African rain forest covers about 386,000 square miles (1 million km²) of

The Gombe Stream National Park occupies a patch of rain forest just 20 sq. mi. (52 km²) in area. It is located in northwestern Tanzania and is famous for its chimpanzees.

KEY FACTS

● **About 5,000 sq. mi. (13,000 km²) of African forest is being cleared each year. Eighty percent of Ghana's original forest cover and 75 percent of Sierra Leone's have already been destroyed.**

● **Firewood gathered from both the original rain forest and replanted areas probably accounts for as much as 75 percent of all energy used in Africa south of the Sahara.**

● **Over 400 species of orchids have been found in western Africa's forests.**

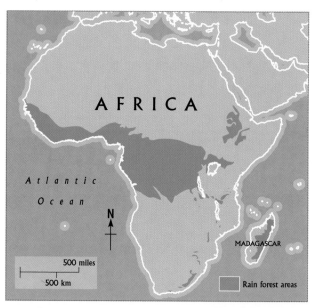

the Congo River basin, a vast network of waterways and swamps that, in prehistoric times, was a large, shallow lake. The basin lands stretch across the Congo Republic, the Democratic Republic of the Congo, Equatorial Guinea, Gabon, and the southern end of Cameroon and the Central African Republic. At its eastern limits, the forest climbs the slopes of the Ruwenzori Mountains on the Uganda border.

The rain forest zone extends into western Africa, forming a strip along the coast of the Gulf of Guinea from Sierra Leone to Nigeria, where it surrounds the delta of the Niger River. Tangled roots of mangrove trees fringe the coasts and estuaries.

Madagascar, off the eastern coast of Africa, also contains a rain forest zone. This large island lies in the Indian Ocean, across the Mozambique Channel, and its surviving rain forests are chiefly in the north and west.

Hunters and Farmers

The oldest inhabitants of central Africa's rain forests are peoples such as the Twa, the Aka, and the Mbuti. Few people understand the rain forest as well as these peoples do. The forest provides them with food in the form of the animals they hunt and the honey and wild plants that they gather. They travel in small bands and build temporary shelters of branches and leaves.

Larger, stockier peoples make up the greatest number of forest dwellers in central Africa. They speak related groups of languages that are known as Bantu or Niger-Congo. Bantu peoples occupy western Africa's forest zone. They have always lived by farming, clearing temporary plots of land from the forest to grow crops such as yams or plantains.

Various rain forest peoples live in Cameroon. Even at a young age, this Mbuti boy is learning to hunt and make good use of forest resources.

Plants and Animals

Africa's rain forests are among the richest sites a naturalist can explore on Earth. They are home to a vast number of flowering plants, from African violets to brilliant blue-and-yellow, sword-leafed *Strelitzias*, or

IN FOCUS

Logging in Cameroon

Cameroon lies on the edge of the Congo River basin, between central and western Africa. It is the third biggest exporter of tropical timber in Africa. Foreign-owned companies run most of its logging operations, and their chief export market is Europe. About 17 percent of the country's 300 tree species are commercially felled. The most important species are hardwood types, often known as African mahogany, including sapele, utile, gedu nohor, and azobe.

bird-of-paradise flowers. A huge variety of climbing plants, creepers, and palm trees flourish here. The oil palm grows to a height of 50 feet (15 m), with glossy green fronds that can reach a length of 15 feet (4.6 m). About 180 large tree species live in the western African rain forest alone. Commercially felled hardwood trees include ebony, iroko, sapele, and okoume.

The animal life of the African rain forests includes gorillas, chimpanzees, colobus monkeys, pygmy hippopotamuses, chameleons, fruit bats, and brilliantly colored tree frogs. Birds such as hornbills and parrots flutter in the rain forest canopy, while the splendid Congo peafowl (a kind of pheasant) struts over the forest floor. Madagascar's rain forest is home to many animals seen nowhere else on Earth, including mammals such as the aye-aye (IE-ie) and a number of lemur species such as the indri.

This red colobus was photographed in Gambia. These shy, leaf-eating monkeys are found across the African forests. In many regions their survival is under threat.

Exploiting the Forests

Like rain forests in other parts of the world, African rain forests are under threat. Deforestation has been extreme in Madagascar, where over three-quarters of the island's forest cover has already been destroyed, and also in large areas of western Africa. Remote forest areas of the Congo River basin have been harder to exploit, but scientists and conservationists are worried about the future of the region as it is opened up to the outside world.

Farming has caused about 70 percent of Africa's deforestation. This includes both the slash-and-burn method of agriculture used by villagers and the clearing of land for large-scale commercial plantations of crops such as oil palms or rubber trees.

As more people are born, the human impact on African forests increases substantially. Many Africans scour the forests to collect wood for household fires or for making charcoal.

Industrial logging has been carried out on an international scale for the last 50 years or so. Eleven countries are members of the African Timber Organization (ATO), which attempts to regulate the logging industry. Even when the amount of timber taken is small, it takes 50 years or more for hardwood trees to grow back and mature.

The large roads cut through the forest to reach and transport old-growth trees bring additional problems. With the roads come hunters in search of food and farmers in search of land. If farmers cultivate the land, there's little chance of the forests growing back again. Surveys have shown that for every mile of logging road built, deforestation and farming devastates more than 13 square miles of forest (1 km of road causes 24 km² of damage). Because of the lack of nutrients in rain forest soil, these farms usually do not succeed.

A Future for the Forests
Within approximately 40 years, it is possible that little rain forest will remain in western Africa and that only patches will remain in the Congo River basin. Destroying this habitat could endanger the survival of many animal and plant species. Over 80 animal species are already threatened in the Democratic Republic of the Congo alone.

What is being done? The International Tropical Timber Organization and governments of countries in the African rain forest zones are all too aware of the scale of the problem. In 2000 in Yaoundé, Cameroon, five African governments agreed to a conservation plan for over 8.6 million

acres (3.5 million ha) of forest across the Congo River basin. National reserves have been created from the Central African Republic to the Democratic Republic of the Congo. However, illegal logging and clearing for farms are difficult to control, particularly where terrain may be remote and countries lack the money to pay rangers to ensure the land is protected. Wars in western Africa and the Congo River basin have worsened these problems, sapping funds and making the forests dangerous to police. Even so, advances in conservation are heartening for the future.

IN FOCUS

Little and Large

Animals of the African rain forest are record breakers in many ways. The gaboon viper (below) sports the longest fangs of any snake in the world. Up to 2 in. (5 cm) long, these fangs can deliver a huge amount of venom. The gigantic goliath frog of western Africa is the biggest frog of all at 2 1/2 ft. (76 cm) long. In contrast, the tiny water chevrotain or mouse deer is just 12 in. (30 cm) high at the shoulder.

Check these out:
- Chimpanzee
- Congo
- Deforestation
- Gorilla
- Homes in the Rain Forest
- Hunter-Gatherer
- Logging
- Madagascar
- Mbuti People
- People of the Rain Forest

Amazonia

Just slightly smaller than Australia, Amazonia is the vast region drained by the Amazon River. The Amazon is by far the world's largest river, only slightly shorter than the Nile in Africa but carrying much more water because of its enormous width. Some of the Amazon's 15,000 tributaries are themselves among the world's largest rivers. Even as far from the sea as Iquitos, Peru, nearly 2,000 miles (3,200 km) inland, the Amazon is still some 4 miles (6.5 km) wide, while in parts of Brazil it reaches the fantastic width of 40 miles (64 km). One-fifth of all the fresh water on Earth is contained within the Amazonian system.

Amazonian Rain Forest

Dense lowland tropical rain forest covers much of Amazonia, the largest area of such forest still

KEY FACTS

● **The source of the Amazon River lies high in the Peruvian Andes at 16,950 ft. (5,168 m).**

● **Amazonia is home to more than 2,000 species of birds—almost a quarter of the world's total.**

● **Some of the Amazon's 15,000 tributaries are themselves among the world's largest rivers.**

remaining anywhere and about half the current world total of rain forest.

Three main types of forest grow in Amazonia. Massive floods along the Amazon every year dictate where each forest lies. Areas that lie above the normal maximum flood level are called *tierra firme* forest,

Flooded igapo forest along the Ariau River near the city of Manaus in Amazonia. The Ariau is a black-water river, stained dark brown by humus.

meaning "hard ground." This type of forest holds the highest number of plant and animal species.

There are two types of seasonal flooded forest. The *varzea* is found along so-called white-water rivers, which carry huge amounts of silt eroded from high in the Andes Mountains. When the floods recede, this silt is left behind in the forest, acting as natural fertilizer and supporting an enormous range of plants and animals.

The second type of seasonal flooded forest, the *igapo* forest, is found along so-called black-water rivers, which are acidic and stained dark brown or black by humus. This type of forest supports less plant and animal life than the other two kinds of forest.

Amazonian Biodiversity

Amazonia probably harbors the world's highest diversity of fauna (animals) and flora (plants). Some 50,000 species of woody plants have already been described, around one-fifth of all those known on Earth. One area of Ecuadorian Amazonia boasts the world's richest variety of trees, with over 100 species per acre (250 per ha). The number of animal species probably runs into the millions, most of which are insects. In one small area of Rondônia, scientists have recorded over 1,800 species of butterflies, while more than 80 species of amphibians are known from another small area. Amazonia is the world's primate capital: it is home to around 45 species of primates, compared with just 30 for all of Africa. Some are still to be discovered.

Damage and Protection

Humans are destroying much of the original forest in Amazonia at an increasing rate for farming, mining, and generating electricity.

Many plants and animals live only in Amazonia. Several of these species are endangered, but very little of the Amazonian area is currently protected in national parks or reserves.

IN FOCUS

A Sarayacu's Song

Amazonia has the world's highest diversity of amphibians. The Sarayacu tree frog is one of the most colorful in the region. It breeds in ponds in both untouched and secondary rain forest within a large area of the Amazonian region. It spends the day hunched down against a leaf, and becomes active at night. The male, which at around 1 in. (28 mm) long is smaller than the female, has a yellow vocal sac. He inflates it like bubblegum when he is calling, which he does from low vegetation in and around the edges of ponds.

Check these out:

- Amphibian
- Biodiversity
- Clear-Cutting
- Deforestation
- Endangered Species
- Fish
- Flooding
- Hydroelectricity
- Marmoset and Tamarin
- Primate
- Rain Forest
- River
- South America

Amphibians are animals that spend the first part of their life cycle in water and the second part out of it. In general the adults spend most of their lives on land, while the young are tadpoles, fishlike larvae that live in water and breathe using feathery gills.

Frogs, toads, salamanders, and caecilians (sih-SIHL-yuhns) are all amphibians. Most adults use their webbed feet for swimming or for gripping moist leaves. Caecilians are like large earthworms, with ring-shaped grooves along their bodies, no legs, and tiny eyes. Their massive skulls push into the earth as they burrow.

Adult amphibians usually have lungs, though rain forest salamanders have none. Many frogs, toads, and salamanders also absorb oxygen through the linings of their large mouths, as well as through their skin.

At Home in the Rain Forest

With their high humidity, rain forests are ideal homes for amphibians. Tiny frogs and salamanders live among the pools of water in between the leaves of bromeliads (broe-MEE-lee-ads) and other plants. Tree frogs climb high into the canopy, clinging to leaves with little suckers on their toes. Salamanders squeeze their long, thin bodies between the roots of trees, under old logs, and in and out of dead leaves in search of prey. Caecilians burrow into the damp forest floor in search of ants, termites, and worms.

The humid atmosphere and damp surroundings prevent amphibians' skin from drying out; it stays moist and sometimes slimy. This helps them absorb oxygen from the atmosphere through their skin and absorb dissolved oxygen from the water as they swim.

Fast Food

The rain forests of the world are teeming with ants, termites, flies, and a host of other insects that amphibians feed upon. Predators, many amphibians hunt by night when conditions are wetter and they are less visible to

Caecilians are legless amphibians. They feed on worms, ants, and termites, and use their massive heads to burrow into the forest floor.

their enemies. Most amphibians feed on insects, worms, slugs, and other small invertebrates, but some of the large frogs and toads, such as the South American horned toad, may eat prey as big as mice. The African clawed toads and the South American pipa toads hunt underwater, lying in wait just below the surface.

Fishlike Young

Amphibians lay soft eggs that dry out easily, but they are often surrounded by a jellylike substance that helps keep them moist. Usually the eggs are laid in water, but rain forest salamanders and some frogs lay them in shady places or in the tiny pools trapped in epiphytes. The eggs will hatch into tadpoles that will need water nearby. Some small forest frogs help their newly hatched tadpoles by carrying them to water on their back.

Tree frogs, such as the glass frog of Central and South America, stick their eggs to leaves overhanging forest pools or slow-moving streams. When they hatch, the tadpoles drop into the water. American nest-building frogs lay their eggs in similar places or at the water's edge. They whip up a froth of foam from water, air, and the mucus around the eggs to camouflage them and to protect them from drying out.

Potent Defenses

Many amphibians are green or brown, well camouflaged against their forest background. Some toads can even change color to match dry or damp leaves.

Other amphibians' skin contains poisons that taste bad or are even lethal. The toxin of the poison dart frogs of South and Central America is so potent that local

Eggs in a Backpack

Not all rain forest amphibians start life as tadpoles. Marsupial frogs of South and Central America press their fertilized eggs into soft patches on the female's lower back, where the skin grows over and protects them. The tadpoles develop inside the liquid-filled eggs and hatch as miniature frogs or toads.

people use it to tip their arrows. Poisonous species often advertise that fact with brilliant red or orange colors to warn off predators.

When threatened, the fire-bellied toads of Asia raise their legs, arch their back, and freeze perfectly still, showing off their brilliant orange bellies. Other frogs also use surprise tactics. The red-eyed leaf frogs of Central and South America flash open their thighs to reveal bright orange-and-black patterns, then make their escape. The South American four-eyed frog turns its back to attackers and puffs up its bottom, which looks like the head of a much larger animal, complete with a pair of huge black "eyes."

Check these out:
- Camouflage
- Frog and Toad
- Insectivore
- Salamander
- Tree Frog

Ant

There are about 15,000 different species, or kinds, of ants in the world. Social insects, all ants live in well-organized colonies where each individual works for the good of the whole community. Hundreds of species live in the rain forests, where they probably outweigh all the other animals living there.

Many rain forest ants nest in the soil or in fallen trees. Some build nests with soil and chewed wood and stick them to tree trunks or branches, out of the way of many predators.

Each colony contains one or more queens and large numbers of wingless females called workers. The workers build the nest, collect all the food, and look after the queen and the young ants. Males are reared only in certain seasons. Equipped with wings, the males fly off to mate with young queens from other colonies, their sole function. While males die soon after mating, the queens usually just lose their wings. Queens do not need their wings because they spend all of their time in the nest laying eggs.

Most rain forest ants live much the same way as ants elsewhere in the world, feeding on a mixture of plant and animal food. However, several special ants with very different lifestyles thrive in the rain forests.

Ferocious Army Ants

Army ants, including legionary and driver ants, live in the forests of South America and Africa. They do not make permanent nests; their colonies are so

Army ants meet in a deep crevice to form a living bridge by linking their bodies together. The other ants in the column then march across the bridge.

IN FOCUS

Ants for First Aid

Army ants have huge jaws, which African forest dwellers use to stitch wounds. They force the ants to bite into both edges of a cut until their jaws meet and pull the wound's edges together. Their heads are then cut off, and the jaws stay firmly closed around the cut until it heals.

big that they have to move their homes quite often. Some army ant colonies contain millions of ants; if they did not move, they would quickly run out of food. Army ants hunt every day, streaming out from their temporary homes in long columns to search the surrounding forest. They feed mainly on other insects, but they will eat any animal that does not get out of their way. Their powerful jaws have reduced caged leopards to skeletons. Known as soldiers, some of the workers are bigger than the others and have extra-large jaws. Their job is to defend the other ants, and they usually march at the edges of the columns.

African driver ants excavate temporary homes in the soil. American legionary ants settle down above ground, where the queen is protected inside a huge ball of workers. The queen is so swollen with eggs that she can hardly move. She has to be carried or dragged along by the workers when the colony moves to a new home.

The male ants are much bigger than the workers and soldiers; they do not look like ants at all. With their soft brown bodies, they are often called sausage flies.

Leaf-Cutting Gardeners

The leaf-cutter ants of South and Central America live in huge underground colonies containing up to 10 million ants. Some of their nests extend more than 15 feet (4.6 m) below ground and may have over 1,000 chambers. The ants may dig out over 22 tons (20 metric tons) of soil and pile it up around their nest. At night worker ants flood out to cut leaves from the surrounding trees and shrubs with their scissorlike jaws. Each one then marches home again, waving a piece of leaf above its head. Workers from one nest can strip the leaves from a whole tree in a few nights.

The ants carry the leaf fragments deep into the nest but do not eat them. Instead, other workers take the fragments, cut them into smaller pieces, then pack them into chambers that serve as gardens. A special kind of fungus grows on the chopped-up leaves, and

Leaf–cutter ants are often called parasol ants because they hold the leaf fragments above their heads. The ants carry pieces of leaf much bigger than their own bodies.

HOW WEAVER ANTS BUILD THEIR NEST

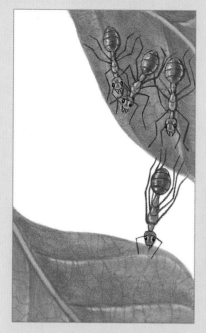

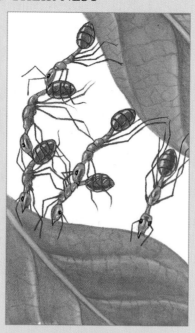

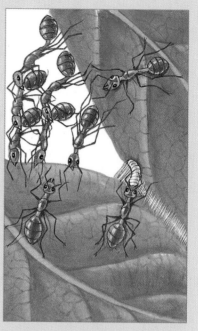

1. Weaver ants build pouchlike nests by fixing leaves together. Gripping the leaf edges with its jaws and back legs, a single ant bridges a small gap and pulls the leaves together.

2. If the gap between the leaf edges is too wide for a single ant, two or more ants may form a chain to bridge the gap and gradually pull the edges together.

3. When the edges have been pulled together, other worker ants arrive with the grubs. When gently squeezed, the larvae give out a silk that glues the leaf edges shut.

the ants feed on the fungus, their only food. Antibiotics secreted by the ants ensure that other kinds of fungi and bacteria do not grow on the gardens and spoil the food. When a young queen goes off on her mating flight, she always takes a little piece of fungus garden with her so that she will have the right fungus in her new nest.

Weaver Ants

Weaver ants live mainly in the forests of Africa and Southeast Asia. They make pouchlike nests by fixing several leaves together—but not by actually weaving them. Instead they glue the leaves together with sticky silk produced by their grubs. When they need to add another leaf or repair any damage, the workers carry the grubs to the site and squeeze

them gently. The glue comes out like toothpaste from a tube.

These ants are carnivorous; they protect the plants on which they live by attacking other insects that try to eat the leaves. Some plants even provide ready-made homes for the ants that protect them. Several kinds of acacia (uh-KAE-shuh) shrubs and trees, for example, have hollow thorns, and the ants make their homes inside these. The plants may also produce food for the ants in the form of nectar or small, fatty beads that ooze from glands on the leaves. In return the ants attack other insects that try to nibble the leaves, including leaf-cutter ants.

Check these out:

- Carnivore
- Fern
- Fungus
- Insect
- Invertebrate
- Nest and Nest Building

The three main kinds of anteaters are all found in Central and South America. The giant anteater lives mainly on open plains, but it occasionally enters all kinds of forests in search of food. The tree anteater or tamandua, although mainly a forest animal, will feed in any habitat where there are plenty of trees—and plenty of termites. The two-toed, or silky, anteater is the only anteater that lives only in tropical forests, from southern Mexico through Central America to northern Peru. Very little is known about this small anteater in the wild, though it is probably still quite common because it exists in such a large area of rain forest.

Specialized Feeders

All anteaters feed in the same way, using their very long tongues, coated in sticky saliva, to probe inside ants' or termites' nests. Their prey becomes stuck on their tongue so when the anteater pulls its tongue back into its mouth, it can swallow a mouthful of ants. Anteaters' thick fur protects them from the painful stings of their prey.

Silky Anteaters

About the size of a squirrel, the silky anteater is an inconspicuous animal. Although it is very widespread, it is rarely seen because it is active only at night, spending most of its life in the trees and only rarely venturing to the ground. The silky anteater specializes in eating ants that live on branches far above the ground and in the stems of lianas (lee-AH-nuhs), plants that hang from the branches of tall trees.

Because of their size, silky anteaters are very vulnerable to predators. If one is threatened, it clings to a branch with its tail and hind legs and holds its front claws over its face. The anteater often feeds in silk cotton trees, where it is camouflaged among the fluffy fruits.

A northern tamandua in the rain forest of Costa Rica. Like all anteaters, its tongue is covered with backward-pointing spines and sticky saliva.

Check these out:
● Ant ● Camouflage ● Insectivore
● Nocturnal Animal

Antelopes are graceful grazing and browsing animals of Africa and Asia. Most live in large herds on the open grasslands, but several have become adapted for life in the African rain forests. These forest antelopes do not live in large herds because the dimly lit forest floor cannot produce enough plant food to support a large group. Instead they live singly or in small groups mainly in and around clearings or on riverbanks, where enough low vegetation grows to eat and to hide in. They often invade newly planted plantations and may damage crops in other cultivated areas.

Forest antelopes are smaller than most of their grassland relatives, with much smaller horns as well. Although generally some shade of brown or gray on the back, their undersides are always much paler. In some species the underside is pure white. This arrangement is called countershading: the pale belly helps counteract the shadow on the underside of the body. This makes

KEY FACTS

● Antelopes belong to the same family (Bovidae) as sheep, goats, and cattle.

● The smallest antelope, the royal antelope, is only 20 in. (50 cm) long and less than a foot (30 cm) tall.

The bongo is the largest of the forest-living antelopes. Its patterned coat makes it hard to spot among the vegetation.

Horns

Most antelopes have horns. Each horn has a bony core covered with horny material like human fingernails. Male antelopes use their horns mainly to fight among themselves for control of the females. The females generally have smaller horns; some lack horns completely. Antelope horns may be straight or curved, but they are never branched. Forest antelopes grow short, straight horns since larger ones would get tangled in the vegetation.

the animal more difficult to see against its background, especially at night.

The Bongo

The largest of the rain forest antelopes is the bongo. Although little more than 3 feet (1 m) high, it is over 6 feet (2 m) in length and can weigh up to 850 pounds (380 kg). With its short, straight horns pointing back over its shoulders, it can easily force its way through dense vegetation. Its striking striped coat provides excellent camouflage. Bongos live in scattered populations throughout the lowland rain forests of Africa but are rarely seen.

Smaller Antelopes

The smallest rain forest antelope is the royal antelope, which lives in the dense forests of western Africa from Sierra Leone to Ghana. About 20 inches (50 cm) long and less than a foot (30 cm) high to the top of its arched back, this is one of the smallest of all hoofed animals. It weighs no more than 6 pounds (2.7 kg). The male's horns are tiny, backward-pointing spikes no more than about an inch (2.5 cm) long, and the female has no horns at

all. Not tall enough to reach many growing leaves, they feed mainly on grass, roots, and fallen fruit. Royal antelopes are shy. Active mainly at night, they rest in thick cover during the daytime. If disturbed, they run off at high speed, twisting this way and that to make it hard for predators to follow them. Surprisingly good jumpers, they can leap up to 10 feet (3 m) in a single bound.

The pygmy antelope is closely related to the royal antelope but is slightly larger. It lives in the dense forests of western and central Africa and behaves just like its smaller cousin. In both species the front legs are shorter than the back ones, so the head is lower than the rest of the body, giving the animals a streamlined shape ideal for plunging through dense vegetation.

Diving Duikers

Sixteen different kinds of duikers (DIE-kuhrs) live in the African forests. They are larger than the royal and pygmy antelopes, with the largest species over 50 inches (130 cm) long and weighing up to 175 pounds (80 kg). Males and females both have short horns. *Duiker* is an Afrikaans name meaning "diver," and it refers to the way in which the animals dive into dense cover when disturbed. Like the royal and pygmy antelopes, they are lower at the front than at the back, and they slip easily through the vegetation. Most duikers are active at night, but some browse in the daytime on leaves, twigs, and bark.

Check these out:
● Africa ● Camouflage ● Congo ● Herbivore ● Mammal ● Nocturnal Animal

Ape

The ape family includes the most highly developed animals on Earth, such as the orangutans, gorillas, chimpanzees, and humans. Except for humans, apes are found only in Africa and Asia; no apes live in the rain forests of Australia or in Central or South America. The superfamily that includes the apes (Hominoidea) also includes gibbons, which are found in Asian forests. All apes can be recognized by their broad chests—almost square in gorillas—and the lack of a tail.

The natural home for all species of wild apes is tropical rain forest, ranging from steamy lowland forests to montane forests on the slopes of African volcanoes, home of the rare and endangered mountain gorilla.

African Apes

Gorillas and chimpanzees live in African rain forests. The biggest of all apes, a male gorilla can reach a weight of 360 pounds (162 kg), compared with an average weight for human males of around 168 pounds (76 kg). Gorillas spend most of their time on the ground, where their food is, in groups of up to 30 or more members. Even the lighter females and juveniles seldom move up into the trees, except at night to build their sleeping nests. Mountain gorillas spend much of their day eating the large amounts of plant food needed to sustain such a bulky animal. They do not mind a few prickles;

Despite their great size and imposing features, gorillas are usually placid animals. This is a male western lowland gorilla.

The chimpanzee is our closest animal relative and is quite intelligent. Here a male is using a large stone to crack open some palm nuts he has gathered.

in fact, giant nettles and thistles are among their favorite foods. Gorillas are usually placid animals and generally get along well together, with few disputes ever breaking out among group members.

Chimpanzees, humans' closest relatives, are much smaller, with the largest males reaching a weight of only about 88 pounds (40 kg). Chimpanzees do all their traveling on the ground but devote much of their day to feeding up in the trees, especially when the trees are heavily laden with ripe fruit. In some areas chimpanzees have turned to hunting monkeys, pigs, and antelopes, and certain groups also fish for termites and ants, poking sticks into their nests to dig out their prey.

The bonobo chimpanzee is only slightly smaller than the chimpanzee and tends to move around in the treetops rather than on the ground, since it is much more agile in leaping and diving from branch to branch. Both species of chimpanzees are highly intelligent, with big, round heads containing relatively large brains.

Asian Apes

Two groups of apes—orangutans and gibbons—live in Asian rain forests. The six species of gibbons are the smallest of the apes, with lanky bodies, long arms, short legs, and hooklike hands and feet. Uniquely among apes, they spend virtually their whole lives up in the rain forest canopy, through which they can move at astonishing speeds using a form of locomotion called brachiation (brae-kee-AE-shuhn). The gibbon races through the canopy, swinging from one branch to the next on its long arms. Gibbons are the noisiest of the apes, often emitting raucous, booming screams and shrieks.

17

Noisy Gibbons

The largest of the gibbons, the siamang (SEE-uh-mang) amplifies its call with an inflatable air sac in its throat. This loud cry makes the sound travel much farther through the dense vegetation in the forest canopy, which acts like a muffler, absorbing much of the sound produced. The female siamang performs the so-called great call in the early morning in a duet with the much softer-voiced male. This song is a kind of vocal bombardment: the callers are advertising their ownership of a territory to their neighbors, which helps give each gibbon group enough feeding grounds to support it.

Orangutans live on the islands of Sumatra and Borneo. They differ slightly in each of their two homes, so two different subspecies have been described. Among apes, orangutans are second in size only to the gorilla, and a large male may reach a weight of 170 pounds (77 kg).

This is about the same weight as the average human male, but orangutans are far stronger. They need those long and strong arms to support their bulky weight in the treetops, for orangutans spend little time on the ground. Orangutans sleep up in the trees, building a temporary nest by bending down a few thin branches to form a cradle. Their diet consists of fruits, young leaves, and shoots, and they regularly eat insects, bark, lianas, mineral-rich soils, and occasionally eggs and small vertebrates. If the opportunity arises, they will eat meat such as baby monkeys or gibbons.

Despite their strong arms, orangutans are simply too heavy to swing easily from tree to tree. Instead they move cautiously around, spreading their weight by always trying to keep at least three of their hands and feet in contact with branches. Orangutans are by far the least sociable of the great apes and dislike the company of other orangutans; mothers, however, will keep one or two of their young near them for a few years until they reach maturity and leave.

An Uncertain Future
The fate of the apes is very much linked to what happens to the rain forests—and these are disappearing at an alarming rate. The apes are generally large primates and so need large areas in which to feed. Setting aside small areas of forest as reserves is useless if the apes within them are to have good prospects for long-term survival.

Check these out:
● Chimpanzee ● Congo ● Endangered Species ● Gibbon ● Gorilla ● Locomotion ● Mammal ● Orangutan ● Primate

Armadillos are little mammals with stout bodies, short legs, a short tail, and a wedge-shaped snout. Heavy, armorlike plates made of bone and horn extend from the end of the armadillo's snout to the tip of its tail. The plates are arranged in overlapping bands, with flexible skin in between, like a pill bug, so the animal can bend. Its underparts are less armored and more flexible.

There are 20 species of armadillos. The smallest is the lesser fairy armadillo, or pink fairy armadillo, which is only 6 inches (15 cm) long. The largest is the rare giant armadillo, 10 times larger and weighing up to 133 pounds (60 kg). Only the nine-banded armadillo and the much rarer giant armadillo regularly live in rain forests.

Armadillos are shy animals, coming out to feed mainly at night. Ants, termites, and other small invertebrates make up most of their diet, plus a little plant material and some carrion.

With powerful claws on their front feet, armadillos dig out burrows to live in. If threatened, they can tunnel in at remarkable speed. The armor plating protects them while they burrow as well as when they are attacked.

Armadillos have several ways of escaping from danger. They can run fast, scampering along on the tips of their front claws and the soles of their hind feet. If there is no time to burrow, they will slash at a predator with their claws. Three-banded armadillos can roll themselves into a tight ball when threatened. Even armadillos that cannot roll up will crouch down so that their armor completely surrounds their softer underparts. Good swimmers, they swallow air to help their heavy bodies float.

While armadillos may be pests in farmers' fields when they burrow under crops, on the whole they are useful animals. They help control insects and, by feeding on carrion, help keep their surroundings clean.

A nine–banded armadillo sniffs the soil to find its prey of insects and small vertebrates, holding its breath as it digs.

Check these out:
- Insectivore
- Mammal
- Nocturnal Animal

The Ashaninka (ah-shah-NIN-kah), also called Campa, live in the tropical rain forest of South America. They are native to the eastern slopes of Peru's Andes Mountains. Their lands lie in the Gran Pajonal region, an area where the rivers and streams form a portion of the headwaters of the vast Amazon River basin.

Heavy rain between October and April creates dense evergreen forests on the mountain slopes and tropical rain forests in the lower elevations. The abundance of wildlife and plant life make it an ideal environment for a hunting and gathering people like the Ashaninkas.

The location of the Ashaninkas placed them far from the centers of power of the great Inca Empire, which dominated the region before the arrival of the Spanish in the 1500s. The Incas tried to conquer the Ashaninkas, but their many small villages

KEY FACTS

● **For centuries the isolation of the Ashaninkas gave them protection from the Incas, the Spanish, and the Peruvians. Today the outside world is forcing great changes upon them.**

● **Ashaninkas' traditional shirts are made from tree bark.**

● **Ashaninka wives are expected to walk behind their husbands and not at their sides.**

were too hard to find and too widely scattered throughout their vast region of dense rain forest.

About a hundred years after the Spanish conquered the Incas, the Spanish began attempting to convert the Ashaninkas to their religion. However, after a number of attempts to establish missions in the Ashaninka homeland, they failed.

The Ashaninkas value community life, with men, women, and children participating in group events.

An Ashaninka woman in ceremonial dress.

Ashaninka Home Life

Palm leaves provide Ashaninkas with their primary building material. An Ashaninka shelter can be constructed quickly, since it consists simply of a palm-thatched roof supported by a few poles. The only furnishings are an elevated sleeping platform at one end and a cooking fire at the other end. Ashaninkas are skilled at fashioning palm leaves into rope, mats for the dirt floor, and many other useful things.

The rain forest once provided the Ashaninkas with all their clothing. Shirts, including their most distinctive traditional garment, a very long shirt dyed red with natural forest dyes, were woven from bark. Today many Ashaninkas have adopted European clothing and wear their traditional garments only for special cultural events.

The Ashaninkas practice polygamy—a man is allowed to have more than one wife—but usually only the leader of a band does this. In Ashaninka family life, men have more power than women. A wife is expected to walk behind her husband, not beside him.

Territory and Independence

The Ashaninkas are not a united political nation. They consist of many different small bands of families that are related to one another. Each band has its own territory that other bands recognize. Within that territory they hunt, gather, and farm, growing yucca, sugarcane, and bananas. Rivalry often arises between Ashaninka groups, which can sometimes lead to one band raiding another one.

The Ashaninka way of life, with villages frequently moving to practice slash-and-burn agriculture, is now being threatened by all the pressures of the dominant civilization. Peruvians have taken determined steps toward extending their authority over Ashaninka country. Permanent settlers have built plantations, where more and more Ashaninkas work for wages.

IN FOCUS

Fancy Weddings

Unlike some Amazon rain forest peoples, such as the Kayapo and the Yanomami, the Ashaninkas have an elaborate wedding ceremony. Based on degrees of kinship, strict rules govern who may marry whom. A bride goes into seclusion for a period of time before the wedding. The wedding itself is an impressive ceremony, a great feast with music.

Check these out:

Asia covers a vast area, from the dry deserts of the Middle East in the west to the sprawling coniferous forests of Siberia in the north and the deciduous forests of the Japanese islands in the east. The rain forests and monsoon forests grow only in the south, from southwest India through southern China and Southeast Asia to the Philippines and Indonesia. The variety of wildlife found in these forests is enormous; some of the greatest biodiversity in the world occurs in parts of Asia. Much of this biodiversity is fast being lost, since certain countries in the region also have some of the world's highest rates of forest destruction.

KEY FACTS

● **Some Asian forests receive more than 156 in. (4,000 mm) of rain every year.**

● **The Atlas moth, one of the world's biggest, is found in the rain forest of Asia.**

● **Thirteen kinds of hornbills, a type of bird, live in Thailand's forests.**

● **More than 200 kinds of bats are found in Asia.**

Monsoon Forests

Monsoon forests once flourished over a broad area of central and northern India up into Nepal and eastward into Burma, northern Thailand, Laos, Vietnam, and southern China. While much reduced, huge tracts still survive, often in protected areas. Monsoon forests have a long dry season, when most of the trees lose their leaves, followed by a lengthy wet season, when rain may fall nonstop for days or even weeks on end. The sudden and very welcome

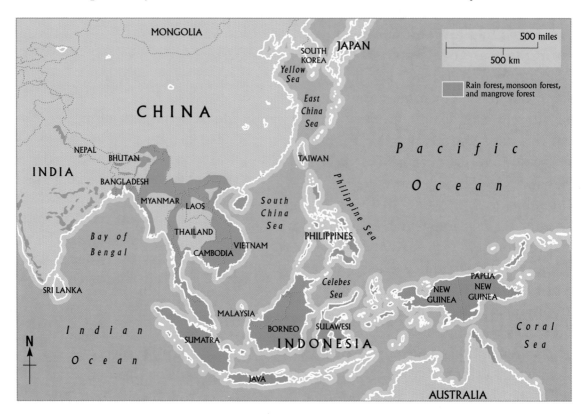

Mount Kinabalu

IN FOCUS

Mount Kinabalu on the island of Borneo is a record-breaker. It is the world's orchid capital, with more than 1,200 species out of the 3,000 or so kinds growing on the island. Mount Kinabalu's forests are damp, and the crooked tree branches are densely clothed in masses of mosses, orchids, and pitcher plants.

arrival of the monsoon rains is the signal for plant and animal life to suddenly explode as the forest awakens from its dry-season slumber.

Rain Forests

In contrast to this startling transformation of the monsoon forests, the rain forests are wet throughout most of the year, presenting the same leafy, dark green face to the world. Rain forests occur sporadically throughout the southern part of Asia, but they are best developed from southern Thailand through Malaysia and much of Indonesia to the Philippines.

Rain forests have a much greater wealth of plants and animals, especially insects, than monsoon forests. The temperatures in the rain forests are also more constant, with fewer extremes. Daytime highs in the rain forest seldom exceed 90°F (32°C), while the Indian monsoon forest can reach 112°F (44°C).

Trees and Flowers

Inch for inch, the tropical rain forests of Asia have the highest biodiversity on Earth. Though they cover only one-third the area of the Amazonian forests, they contain about half the number of species found there. Plant life in the Asian rain forests is diverse and distinctive. Palms flourish in confusing variety, with over 1,300 species in the region. Many of the palms are very spiny climbers, called rattans. Local people use the leaves to make furniture, and they eat the fruits. Rain forest trees grow in much greater variety and much larger sizes than in monsoon forests, with huge buttress roots supporting their enormous trunks. Dipterocarp trees, with their somewhat indigestible leaves, dominate many Asian rain forests and do not occur outside the region. Where dipterocarps are dominant, animals tend to be scarce, since this type of forest simply cannot support a large number of individuals.

All 14 species of rafflesia, or rotting corpse flowers (the world's largest flowers), are restricted to Southeast Asia. The fleshy flower emits an unpleasant smell and, in the largest species, reaches a diameter of more than 3 feet (1 m). The plant is firmly attached to the liana, in which it develops as a parasite. Another group of plants characteristic of the Asian forests are the pitcher plants (unrelated to the American plants of the same name) that rarely live outside of Asia.

Animals of Asia

Asia's animal life is rich and varied. Most of the Asian animal species are related to those of the Afro-tropical region. In terms of numbers, though, Asia has many more species than Africa. For example, more than 1,650 species of birds live in Asia, compared with Africa's 1,500 species.

Several distinct groups of animals are restricted to Asia. Among these are the flying lizards. These do not really fly but glide swiftly from tree to tree, spanning gaps of as much as 165 feet (50 m) by expanding a frill of skin around their bodies, like miniature hang gliders. The

The head of a reticulated python, one of the world's largest snakes. This species lives in the forests of Southeast Asia and Indonesia.

around its head. It spends most of its time in the trees but comes down to the ground to drink and feed on the salty soil that supplements its omnivorous diet.

Around eight species of deer graze in the monsoon and rain forests of Asia; the largest is the sambar. Found in most forest types from India to Taiwan and the Philippines, the sambar is the tiger's favorite prey. In some areas packs of rare, native wild dogs attack sambars as well. The most striking of the deer is the spotted deer, or chital, of India and Sri Lanka. It prefers the open grassy areas within the monsoon forests, where many thousands may gather at certain times.

world's largest snake, the reticulated python, is found only here, as is one of the world's largest poisonous snakes, the king cobra.

The Asian forests, both monsoon and rain forest, are still home to many large animals, such as Asian elephants, three species of rhinoceroses, tigers, leopards, and several species of wild cattle. The variety of primates found in Asia is relatively enormous, from macaques and leaf monkeys to orangutans. The pig-tailed macaque, which ranges from India to Southeast Asia, has a short curly tail. Although it spends more time on the ground than most macaques, local people have taught it to climb coconut trees and gather the nuts. The toque macaque of Sri Lanka is one of the smallest macaques and has become tame in some areas. It will sometimes groom the common langur (another monkey), which is found in most monsoon forests in India and Nepal. The lion-tailed macaque of India's southern rain forests has a mane of pale golden fur

Flying Squirrels

IN FOCUS

Some of the most striking Asian animals are the squirrels. There are dozens of species, including some of the world's largest. Flying squirrels sleep during the day in hollow trees and emerge at dusk to make impressive flights of as much as 1,000 ft. (300 m) from tree to tree in the darkened forest. They do not have wings but instead glide on a membrane that expands between their front and hind feet.

Check these out:

- Biodiversity ● Carnivorous Plant
- Cobra ● Deer ● Elephant ● Indonesia
- Mangrove Forest ● Monsoon Rain Forest
- Orangutan ● Orchid ● Palm Tree
- Rafflesia ● Rain Forest ● Rattan
- Snake ● Squirrel ● Tiger

Although strictly speaking a very large island, Australia is big enough to be regarded as a continent in its own right. Australia is the smallest and flattest continent and also the driest, but it is unique in terms of its wildlife, little of which is found elsewhere.

Ancient Rain Forests

Australia's tropical and subtropical rain forests are confined to Queensland and the northern

KEY FACTS

● **Over the last 200 years, settlers have destroyed three-quarters of Australia's rain forests.**

● **More than 80 percent of Australia's plants and animals are found nowhere else in the world.**

● **Australian rain forests are home to about one-third of the continent's frogs, one-fifth of its birds, one-fourth of its reptiles, one-third of its marsupials, and two-fifths of its plants.**

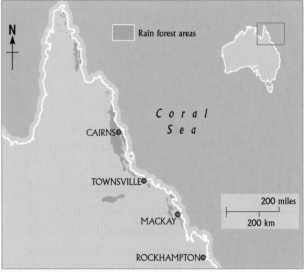

section of New South Wales, in the east and northeast of the continent. Existing for over 100 million years, these are probably the oldest rain forests on Earth. In prehistoric times rain forests may have covered all of Australia, but gradually they naturally retreated to a mere 1 percent. Today rain forest covers a meager 0.3 percent, the result of destruction by people. However, this tiny fragment is a treasure trove of extraordinary riches.

Australian rain forests are home to about one-third of the continent's frogs,

Subtropical rain forest with buttressed trees in Tamborine National Park, Queensland, Australia.

one-fifth of its birds, one-fourth of its reptiles, one-third of its marsupials (kangaroos, wallabies, possums, etc.), and two-fifths of its plants. These occur in different kinds of rain forests, from lowland to mountain, which often give way to drier eucalyptus forests, so that an interesting mix of plants and animals live side by side. It is fortunate that after years of dispute between conservationists and developers, during which much of the forest came perilously close to being bulldozed, the bulk of Queensland's priceless rain forest is now protected as part of a Wet Tropics World Heritage Area.

Rain Forest Animals

The largest animal found in the Australian rain forests is, surprisingly enough, a bird: the 6-foot- (2-m-) high cassowary, which has a spectacular red-and-blue, bare-skinned neck. Like the ostrich, emu, and rhea, the cassowary is flightless. It spends the day stomping around in the forest looking for fallen fruit, its main food. It has a formidable reputation as a fighter when cornered and can reputedly kill a person with one hefty kick from its huge, heavily clawed feet.

Skinks are the most common type of lizard in Australia. A Murray's forest skink stands halfway out of the dead rain forest tree in which it lives.

The rain forest floor is also home to the muskrat kangaroo, an interesting species that scientists regard as a link between the possum and the kangaroo. Like many of the smaller kangaroos, it is active in the daytime, when it can be heard scratching around among the dead leaves, searching for insects and seeds to eat. After dark any scuffling sounds in the leaf litter will probably be made by bandicoots, rabbitlike marsupials that can be common in the rain forests.

IN FOCUS

Eungella National Park

Eungella National Park is named after an aboriginal word meaning "Land of Clouds." One of many national and state parks that protect the remaining rain forests, it has been cut off from other rain forest areas for some 30,000 years; as a result, it now boasts several kinds of plants and animals unique to the area. Of these, the one most easily seen is the Mackay tulip oak, a tall rain forest tree with strong buttress roots supporting the base. The Eungella honeyeater (a bird) may be glimpsed as it flits around in the rain forest understory, searching for insects and flower nectar. The orange-sided skink (a kind of lizard) is similar to many other local skinks. The most unusual of Eungella's unique animals is the gastric brooding frog, which holds its eggs in its stomach until the tadpoles are fully developed, when they are spat out.

Check these out:
- Bird • Deforestation • Frog and Toad
- Indonesia • Mammal • Possum • Rain Forest • Reptile

Bacteria are tiny, single-celled organisms far too small to see with the naked eye, yet most life in the rain forest depends on them. Some are single round cells or rods, while others group together to form chains of cells. With no nucleus or true chromosomes, they are very simple forms of life. Most bacteria have some kind of cell wall, often covered in a coat of slime that helps the bacteria glide over moist surfaces. Some bacteria have tiny, whiplike hairs (flagella) that beat to propel them along.

Bacteria are everywhere in the rain forest—in soil, pools, and puddles; in moisture on leaves and tree trunks; and on and in the bodies of animals. They feed on living or dead plant and animal tissues by oozing digestive juices (enzymes) onto their food (rotting organic material or living plants or animals) to dissolve it, then absorbing nutrients through their cell walls. While invertebrate animals break down the rotting vegetation and the remains of dead animals into smaller pieces, bacteria finish the job, releasing nutrients back into the soil to feed more plants.

Bacteria can multiply very rapidly just by splitting in two. Some can double their numbers every 20 minutes. Occasionally they may form tough spores that are carried to new places on the wind or in water.

Streptomyces bacteria are common in soil and produce long chains of spores. Some species are sources of streptomycin and other antibiotics.

While some bacteria cause diseases such as typhoid, cholera, and salmonella, many are beneficial and help animals to digest their food. Grazing animals such as deer, rabbits, and okapis (which are related to giraffes) have special pouches in their guts that contain millions of bacteria to digest the tough cellulose in plant cell walls and release its nutrients. Even termites have populations of bacteria that help them digest the wood they tunnel through.

In poor soils, especially where heavy tropical rains quickly wash nutrients out of the ground, blue-green bacteria are important providers of nitrates, essential for plant growth. Legumes—plants of the pea family—have special nodules (little lumps) on their roots that house nitrogen-fixing bacteria. Many carnivorous plants, such as pitcher plants and bladderworts, rely partly on bacteria to break down the insects they trap.

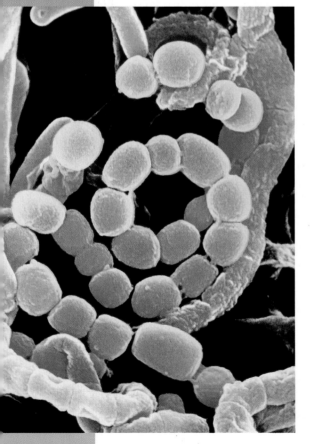

Check these out:
- ● Carnivorous Plant   ● Decomposer   ● Deer
- ● Disease   ● Feeding   ● Food Web   ● Herbivore
- ● Nutrient Cycle   ● Parasite   ● Termite

Bat

Bats are the only mammals that can really fly, although a number of other mammals have flaps of skin that permit them to glide for short distances. Most of the world's bats live in tropical or subtropical regions, and many dwell in the rain forest.

There are two quite separate groups of bats, the microbats and the megabats. Recently scientists realized that these two groups are not closely related to one another. There are over 900 species of bats; 150 of these are megabats, and the rest are microbats.

The main difference between the megabats and the microbats is that megabats do not use echolocation to find their way in the dark, and have good night vision. The oldest of the bats, in terms of when they evolved, are the microbats. They live all over the world, except in the very coldest regions. All North American and European bats are microbats. Both groups of bats are found in rain forests, including most megabat species.

IN FOCUS

Bats by the Millions

Several million bats, of up to eight different species, are known to roost during the day in certain caves in Borneo's rain forest. They come out each night, thousands of them every minute in a continuous stream, to go hunting for food among the forest trees. These bats probably catch and eat several tons of insects from the rain forest each night.

Microbats

The body length of the microbats varies. The smallest, Kitti's hog-nosed bat from Thailand, measures just over 1 inch (3 cm), while the largest, the false vampire bat from South America, grows to nearly 6 inches (16 cm) long. Microbats roost singly, in small groups, or, in the case of some of the Asian rain forest species, in thousands or even millions. Being nocturnal, sight is not really important to microbats; they find their way around using a form of radar called echolocation. They produce high-pitched sounds that bounce off objects around them as they fly. The returning sounds are picked up by the bats' sensitive ears, and the bats can then figure out the size and position of the object they are approaching.

Carnivorous Bats

Many microbats are carnivorous. Besides eating insects, tropical microbats feed on nectar, fruit, small mammals, birds, lizards, frogs, and even fish. One unusual species is the bulldog or fishing bat, which is able to detect a fish moving at the water's surface and can then snatch it up with the strong claws on its hind feet.

Vampire bats are cleverly adapted to feed on blood. They have blunt faces and pointed upper front teeth. These microbats use their razor-sharp teeth to chisel a small cut in their prey's skin. They do this so carefully and gently that the animal does not even feel it happening. The bat then dribbles saliva onto the wound to stop the blood from clotting and drinks the blood by lapping it up with its tongue. Vampire bats have very short tails and longer legs than other bats. This enables them to walk along the ground or on branches to get to their prey.

Vampire bats live only in Central and South American rain forests. There are three species of vampire bats: the common vampire, the white-winged vampire, and the hairy-legged vampire. They roost during the day in caves or hollow trees. Male and female common vampire bats roost separately. The females form groups of 8 to 12 individuals that share food with one another, making sure that if one or more are unable to find food, they at least get something from the others. The males do not form such stable groups; instead they compete with one another for the groups of females. Hairy-legged vampire bats live either singly or in small groups of both sexes, while white-winged vampire bats form colonies in which male and female pairs roost together

A fishing bat trails its sharply-clawed feet into the water of a forest pool as it attempts to catch a fish swimming near the water's surface.

A group of Honduran white bats huddle together in their "tent," formed from a banana leaf.

a short distance from their neighbors. Both of these bat types feed mainly on the blood of birds rather than larger animals like the common vampire bat does.

Only the common vampire bat is known to bite humans. People who live in vampire bat areas have good reason for being afraid of them for, besides drinking their blood, some of them also carry rabies, a potentially fatal disease. As a result, rain forest people often kill any large bats that they see. Vampire bats, however, are quite small, and sadly the bats that are usually killed are harmless, often quite rare species, whose numbers in the wild are falling as a result. The common vampire bat, on the other hand, has increased in numbers as rain forest has been cut down and replaced by ranches. This has provided them with a large source of blood from horses, cattle, and other domestic animals.

Megabats
The megabats include the largest bats, the flying foxes, so-called because of their long muzzles and foxlike faces. The largest species has a body length of 17 inches (43 cm) and a huge wingspan of 5½ feet (1.7 m). Not all megabats are this big, and indeed some of them are smaller than the largest of the microbats.

Megabats are animals of the tropical regions but are not found in the Americas. Like the microbats, they feed at night, but they cannot use echolocation. Instead they have large eyes and, like cats, can see clearly on all but the darkest of nights. The smaller megabats may roost in caves, but not so the larger species. During the day they roost,

IN FOCUS

The Fringe-Lipped Bat

The South American fringe-lipped bat feeds on lizards and frogs, which it catches with its hind feet, just like an osprey or fish eagle does. It hears male frogs when they are calling for females and is able to tell the difference between the calls of those frogs that are poisonous and those that are not.

31

A Queensland tube-nosed bat feeds on a fruit. As its name implies, this megabat lives in the rain forest areas of Queensland in northeastern Australia.

often by the thousands, in the tops of rain forest trees, where they look like dense masses of fruit.

Fruit Bats

Most of the megabats eat fruit, and large numbers of them will gather on particular forest trees as the fruits ripen. The bats hang on to the fruit by the claws on their wings and then use their flattened cheek teeth to crush it. Sometimes they may just drink the juice and spit out the pulp and seeds; other times they will eat the whole fruit. The pulp is then digested, and the seeds are passed out in the droppings. In this way fruit bats are important in dispersing seeds of rain forest trees far and wide.

Short-tailed fruit bats from Central and South America are microbats that are particularly fond of the fruits of a specific type of tree and help disperse their seeds— although they also feed on insects and nectar when fruit is in short supply. In the same forests and with similar tastes in food are the tent-building bats, also microbats. These little bats cut a line with their teeth along either side of the midrib of a large leaf, such as a banana leaf, so that it droops down on either side like a tent. They then hang beneath it in groups of between 2 and 50, not just to sleep but also to escape the regular heavy downpours of the rain forest.

Check these out:
● Canopy ● Carnivore ● Cave ● Central America ● Ecology ● Ecosystem ● Flowering Plant ● Fruit ● Insectivore ● Mammal ● Nocturnal Animal ● Pollination ● Seed

Of the nine species of bear, five live in the rain forests—three in tropical rain forests and two in temperate rain forests. North American temperate rain forests are home to the black bear, which is much more common than most people realize. It regularly fishes in forest streams and feeds from fruiting bushes in autumn. The grizzly bear inhabits the temperate rain forest along the southern coast of Alaska.

Tropical Bears

The only South American bear is the spectacled bear. It lives in the Andes Mountains from western Venezuela to Bolivia. While the spectacled bear prefers humid forests, it also roams the high grasslands up to 14,000 feet (4,200 m), as well as scrubby deserts down to sea level. Human activity threatens all these habitats, and the spectacled bear is listed as a vulnerable species.

Spectacled bears get their name from the circles of white hair around their eyes; the rest of their coat is black. They grow to about 6 feet (1.8 m) long, and males weigh as much as 440 pounds (200 kg). Females are much lighter, up to about 145 pounds (65 kg). Their small size and strong, hooked claws make them good climbers, able to move high into the trees in search of fruit. They also eat insects and carrion. Local people accuse them of taking young domestic stock such as small calves and young goats.

The sun bear of Southeast Asia is the world's smallest bear, growing to just over 3 feet (1 m) long and weighing about 110 pounds (50 kg). Feeding mainly on fruits such as cocoa pods and on the growing tips of palm trees, it may also eat termites and even small mammals and birds. It has been known to damage cocoa and coconut crops. Farmers kill bears for this offense, and because of this as well as the loss of its habitat, it is listed as critically endangered.

The sloth bear lives in eastern India and Sri Lanka. Males can grow to nearly 6 feet (1.8 m) long and weigh about 220 pounds (100 kg). Females are about four-fifths the size of males. The sloth bear is omnivorous, eating everything from sugarcane and honey to eggs, carrion, fruit, and flowers, but especially termites. It has a long, bare snout with nostrils that it can close and a gap where two of its top front teeth would normally be in other bears. After it has broken open a termite mound, it can close its nostrils to keep out the dust, blow away the debris, and suck up the termites through the tube formed by its lips.

The sloth bear of Asian rain forests. It feeds on virtually anything it can find, but is especially fond of termites.

Check these out:
● Carnivore ● Herbivore ● Insectivore ● Mammal ● Nocturnal Animal ● North America ● Rattan

Bees and wasps include many social-insect species that live in large colonies, but the majority live alone. Most of them carry stingers and taste unpleasant, advertising this with bold warning colors, often black and yellow. Bees and social wasps use their stingers to defend themselves and their nests, while the solitary wasps use theirs for paralyzing prey. Only female bees and wasps can sting.

KEY FACTS

● Bees are usually much hairier than wasps. Their hairy coats pick up pollen when they visit flowers.

● The biggest bees are almost as big as some hummingbirds. The smallest ones, often stingless worker bees, are little more than one-twelfth of an inch (2 mm) long.

● Only female bees and wasps can sting; their stinger is a modified part of their egg-laying apparatus.

Social Structure

Bee and wasp colonies have a social structure in which different groups do different jobs. Each colony contains one or a few queens that rule the whole colony by means of pheromones—chemical messages—that ensure that the workers do the right things at the right time. The majority of the insects in the colony are workers, which are all female. Males, called drones if they are honeybees, make up only a small percentage of the population. Males do no work; their sole function is to mate with new queens.

A South American paper wasp chews up the remains of an insect before feeding it to one of the grubs in the nest. The empty cells around the edge of the nest are waiting to receive eggs.

Feeding and Flowers

Adult bees and wasps feed largely on nectar, although some wasps also eat carrion or attack live insects. The main difference between the two groups is in the way they rear their grubs, or larvae. Bees feed their grubs pollen and nectar, but wasp grubs are carnivorous. They feed mainly on insects or spiders provided by their mothers or older sisters. Solitary wasps pack their nests with enough paralyzed prey to last throughout the grubs' lives, while social species feed their grubs regularly with chewed-up insects.

Most bees collect pollen and nectar from a wide variety of flowers, but some bees depend on just one kind of flower; the flowers, in turn, also depend on these particular kinds of bees for pollination. When a bee enters a flower, it can only escape by squeezing past the stamens and picking up pollen, with which it will later pollinate another flower. Many tropical orchids attract these bees with their strong scents and amazing shapes and colors. Some male bees even put the orchids' scents to their own use; they pick up the oily perfume on their hairy legs to become attractive to the females.

Stingless Bees

Stingless bees are not actually stingless, but their stings are too small to hurt people. About 300 kinds live in the Tropics, especially in South America, although not all of them live in the rain forests.

Stingless bees are social insects, forming long-lived colonies that may contain nearly 200,000 workers. They build nests in tree holes, in the ground, or attached to large branches. A protective layer composed of wax, resin, and mud encloses each nest. The bees collect the resin from damaged trees. They carry the resin and mud to the nest in their pollen baskets. These are containers formed by rows of stiff hairs on the back legs of workers. Stingless bees build the cells inside the nest with wax and resin, but although the cells may form vertical or horizontal combs, they are not neatly fitted together

Carpenter Bees

The biggest bees feeding from rain forest flowers are various carpenter bee species. Many have shiny black or purple bodies, often with yellow bands and dark wings. Some of these spectacular insects are over 1 1/2 in. (35 mm) long, with wingspans of over 2 in. (55 mm). They get their name because they nest in deep burrows that they excavate in tree trunks and other wood.

like those of the honeybee. Narrow chimneys of resin often surround the nest entrances, and these possibly prevent other insects from getting in to steal the honey.

Forest-living people regularly break open the nests to take the stored honey, but this is not always painless. Although the bees cannot sting, their sharp jaws can inflict painful bites. The rain forests of Africa and Southeast Asia also contain several wild honeybees similar to those that people keep in hives. Their nests contain large stores of honey, and people readily put up with the stings in order to harvest this food.

These social wasps have attached their nest to the underside of a leaf. The fibers that make up their papery nest are clearly visible.

Nests of Mud and Paper

Most solitary wasps build their nests with mud. Some build in the ground or inside hollow stems, some make neat little pots, while others merely stick lumps of mud on to rocks and tree trunks. They stock each nest with paralyzed prey before sealing it closed. In tropical Asia the *Zethus* wasp chews up leaves and then glues the pieces together with saliva and resin to make a ball-shaped nest containing several chambers. Hanging among the other leaves, these nests are very hard to see.

Social wasps, which include the familiar yellow jackets, build with paper that they make themselves by chewing up dead wood and mixing it with saliva. Yellow jackets live mainly in temperate parts of the world, but many other social wasps with similar habits live in the rain forests. Some of their nests are quite simple, often consisting of just one flat sheet of paper cells hanging from a branch. There is often more than one queen in a colony, although one queen usually lays most of the eggs. The colonies may survive from year to year, and the nests of some species become huge. When a nest gets too big, one or more queens fly off with a group of workers to start a new colony somewhere else.

Wasps and Other Animals

Wasps do not generally attack anyone unless they feel their nest is threatened. The tiger hornet, so-called because of the broad orange stripe on its black body, is one of the biggest and most feared wasps of Southeast Asia. It nests in tree stumps and other low-level sites. Anyone getting too close can be badly stung; people have died after being attacked by these wasps.

However, some animals know how to get the better of wasps. Capuchin monkeys in tropical America get nearly half of their food by mounting lightning raids on small hornet nests. Snatching a nest from a branch, the raider bounds away with it at high speed, leaving most of the hornets buzzing around the empty space. The monkey can then safely feast on the hornet grubs.

Several birds even rely on wasps for protection. The caciques (kuh-SEEKS) of tropical America usually build their nests close to wasps' nests, where few enemies would risk attacking them.

Check these out:
- Flowering Plant ○ Insect ○ Invertebrate
- Nest and Nest Building ○ Pollination

Beetle

Beetles make up nearly a quarter of all the different species of animals living in the world today. They include ladybugs, stag beetles, dung beetles, leaf beetles, weevils, fireflies, and many others, divided into over 150 families. Over 350,000 kinds of beetles have already been discovered, and thousands more are undoubtedly still unknown, especially in the rain forests. One scientist from the Smithsonian Institution's National Museum of Natural History found 1,200 species of beetles living among the branches of just one kind of rain forest tree in Panama. Basing their calculations on this discovery and on the numbers of different trees in the rain forests, some biologists believe there could be several million different kinds of beetles in the world.

KEY FACTS

● Beetles are the most wide-ranging feeders of all insects; there is almost nothing that they cannot eat with their strong jaws.

● Beetles include the heaviest of all insects, but they also include some of the smallest—less than half a millimeter long.

● Over 1,200 species of beetles were found living on just one kind of rain forest tree in Panama.

Tough Wing Cases

Beetles belong to the order Coleoptera. This name means "sheath wings" and refers to the tough front wings that cover most of their body. Known as elytra, these coverings do not really look like wings at all. They are often smooth and brightly colored, meeting in the middle. Most beetles have a pair of delicate hind wings folded neatly under the elytra. These are used for flying, although many beetles are reluctant to fly.

Protected by their elytra and a tough outer skeleton over the rest of their body, beetles can live in the ground and in many other places where more delicate

The bright colors of this South American click beetle warn predators that it is unpleasant to eat. The beetle is laying its eggs on a log, where its grubs will feed on the wood.

This Peruvian tortoise beetle is guarding her eggs. Not many predators are likely to attack her because of her bright warning colors.

vegetarians, munching their way through leaves, flowers, and other parts of plants. Vegetarian beetles can be serious pests in the forest. The larvae of some of them spend several years munching their way through solid wood.

Great Variety

The greatest variety of beetles live in the Tropics. They live at all levels in the rain forests, from the sunlit canopy to the dark floor, and they come in a truly amazing variety of shapes and colors. Many are superbly camouflaged on bark or leaves, while others warn predators of their poisonous nature by displaying conspicuous colors and patterns.

insects would not survive. The space between the elytra and the body can also act like an oxygen cylinder, providing air for water beetles.

Biting Jaws

Young and adult beetles generally have strong biting jaws, and although some of them lap up nectar and the sweet sap that oozes from trees, most of them eat solid food. Some are predators, feeding on a wide variety of other invertebrates. Others are scavengers, beetles that play an important role in cleaning up all sorts of dead and decaying matter. Still others are

The long-horned beetles, of which there are over 20,000 species, are particularly common in the tropical forests. They get their name for their antennae, which are usually longer than their body—in some species as much as five times as long. Their grubs nearly all feed on wood. Most long-horned beetles tunnel in dead and dying timber, but some are serious pests of living trees. The adult beetles are usually camouflaged; some that live on tree trunks have elytra that are hard to distinguish from the surrounding mosses. Some species are brightly colored, including the South American harlequin beetle with its gaudy orange-and-black elytra. This beetle is also remarkable for the male's

Fiddle Beetles

The fiddle or violin beetles, named for their long necks, are odd-looking beetles found mainly on tree trunks in Indonesia. They live on and under bark and, despite being up to 4 in. (10 cm) long, their flattened brown bodies are remarkably hard to see. Their long necks enable them to extract other insects from deep bark crevices.

extremely long front legs, which he uses to guard the female while she lays her eggs.

Stag beetles get their name because most of the males have enormous jaws, often resembling the antlers of a stag. The jaws of the imperial stag beetle from New Guinea are longer than its body. Stag beetles look frightening, but the jaws are used only to wrestle with other males; they cannot bite because their muscles are not strong enough to work these great jaws. Stag beetle grubs feed on dead and decaying wood and play a major role in recycling fallen tree trunks into nutrients that can be used by other plants.

Beetle Enemies

Beetles have many enemies in the rain forest. Chameleons snatch them up with long, sticky tongues. Galagos, tarsiers, and many monkeys—all primates—frequently dine on crunchy beetles, and so do many birds, including the colorful

This Australian chafer beetle is one of many species that chew rain forest flowers.

motmots of South and Central America. Woodpeckers dig juicy beetle grubs from the trees, as do many indigenous rain forest people. Throughout the rain forests, beetles are always at the mercy of ants, especially the voracious army ants of Africa and South America, which can quickly tear a beetle to pieces.

Horned Giants

The world's biggest beetles live in the rain forests. The heaviest of all is the goliath beetle from Africa. As big as a human's fist, it weighs over 3½ ounces (100 g) and is the world's heaviest insect. Some beetles are longer than the goliath, but they are more slender and do not weigh as much. The goliath is one of the huge group of plant-eating beetles called chafers: it uses the short horns on its head to rip open juicy stems. It flies with difficulty, making a loud buzzing noise.

Even more striking are the hercules beetles from the rain forests of tropical America. The male beetle has a large, upward-curving horn on its head and an even larger one arching

The three-horned rhinoceros beetle from Borneo is one of the most bizarre of all beetles. Two of its enormous horns spring up from the top of its head, and a third curves up from below.

forward from its thorax. Including the horns, these beetles are almost 7 inches (18 cm) long. The male hercules beetle uses these horns to fight with other males over territory; during these battles each beetle tries to grab the other one and throw it onto its back. The loser usually stumbles away, leaving the winner to mate with any females in the area. These giant beetles grow up in dead tree trunks and branches. They are also called rhinoceros beetles, although this name is also given to several other kinds of horned beetles in various parts of the world. The true

rhinoceros beetle is a serious pest of coconut palms in Africa and Southeast Asia. Its grubs tunnel into the leaf base and allow decay to set in.

Living Jewels

The bullet-shaped jewel beetles include some of the most colorful of all insects. The brilliant greens, blues, reds, and purples of their elytra change according to the direction the light strikes them. Indigenous rain forest people commonly use these elytra as brooches, necklaces, and even earrings. There are over 12,000 species of jewel beetles. Most of them live in the rain forests, where their tadpolelike larvae usually tunnel in or just under tree bark.

Firefly Trees

Fireflies are night-flying beetles that attract their mates with flashing lights. Chemical reactions in the insects' bodies produce the light. Each species produces and responds only to its own pattern of flashes, so the insects do not attract mates of the wrong species.

In the mangrove swamps of Malaysia and Indonesia, fireflies create the most spectacular display. As darkness falls, a few insects begin to flash. The lights attract other fireflies, and large numbers gradually gather in one particular tree or in a clump of neighboring trees.

Tortoise Beetles

Many tortoise beetles sport shiny gold-and-silver patterns; when they are clinging to leaves, it is difficult to tell them from raindrops glinting in the sunshine. They get their name because the elytra and the thoracic shield, a broad shield or plate just behind the head, extend well beyond the body and look like the shell of a tortoise. Their bright colors usually fade when they die.

Somehow they manage to synchronize their high-speed flashing, and thousands of tiny lights are switched on and off together. The whole tree flashes like a Christmas tree. Only the males of this species produce light. Unmated females in the area see the display and fly there to find a mate.

Check these out:

- Bioluminescence ● Decomposer ● Food Web ● Forest Floor ● Herbivore ● Insect
- Invertebrate

Biodiversity

Biodiversity, or biological diversity, describes the huge variety to be found in nature. It includes all the animal, plant, and microbe species on Earth as well as the special places where they live, known as ecosystems, and the living processes of which they form a part, known as ecological processes.

What is a Species?

The rain forests are the earth's main storehouses of plant, animal, and microbe species. A species consists of many individuals that all share certain characteristics and that normally breed only with one another. However, there are also differences within species. For example, the brown lemur (LEE-muhr) from Madagascar is divided into seven subspecies, each of which looks quite different from the others. In fact at first glance, it appears they are all different species.

The number of species of plants, animals, and microbes on Earth is unknown. Estimates range from about 5 million to 30 million, with some scientists going as high as 100 million, although so far only about 1.4 million have been described.

BIODIVERSITY IN MADAGASCAR

Indri

Diademed Sifaka

Panther Chameleon

Parson's Chameleon

One thing is certain: of all the living creatures found on the world's land areas, by far the great majority of species live only in tropical rain forests. The current total stands at about 50 percent of the plants and animals so far described. If all the creatures that are believed to exist in the rain forests but have yet to be discovered are added to this total, the ratio leaps up to around 90 percent.

Scientists now believe that rain forests have such high biodiversity because of the relatively constant warm temperatures and the abundance of water. This means that evolution into different species can continue year-round, without being interrupted by a long winter break. Scientists also believe that the rain forests have flourished over millions of years, allowing for coevolution—symbiotic animals and plants developing together—to occur, thus resulting in increasingly diverse species.

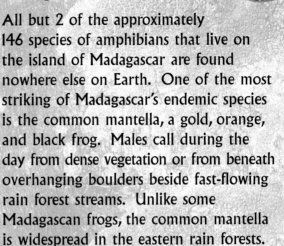

Madagascan Amphibians

All but 2 of the approximately 146 species of amphibians that live on the island of Madagascar are found nowhere else on Earth. One of the most striking of Madagascar's endemic species is the common mantella, a gold, orange, and black frog. Males call during the day from dense vegetation or from beneath overhanging boulders beside fast-flowing rain forest streams. Unlike some Madagascan frogs, the common mantella is widespread in the eastern rain forests.

Staggering Statistics

Whatever the reasons, the facts and figures are truly staggering. The richest temperate forest found in North America, even though covering a vast area, contains about 50 to 60 species of trees. Yet even the poorest of tropical rain forests could manage a similar total in an area the size of a couple of soccer fields. A similar-sized area of rain forest near Iquitos in Peru contains the amazing sum of 300 species of trees. This is nearly one-third higher than the previous record held by an equivalent patch of forest in Borneo. The tiny island of Barro Colorado in Panama contains around 1,370 species of native flowering plants and ferns, one-seventh of the number found in the entire continental United States, which is 625,000 times larger.

Similar astounding statistics apply to the animals of the Tropics. More species of land birds breed in the tiny Central American country

Red-Beilled Lemur

Red-Fronted Lemur

Golden Frog

of Costa Rica than in the United States and Canada combined. Around 90 species of frogs and toads can be counted in a few square miles of Peruvian rain forest, exceeding the total for the continental United States. The crown of a single mighty Amazonian tree can contain more than 50 species of ants, more than occur in all of England, which is the size of the state of Mississippi. As for butterflies, single sites in Peruvian or Brazilian Amazonia hold nearly three times the combined total for North America and Europe.

Regional Biodiversity

Biodiversity is not spread out equally among the world's rain forests. South and Central America probably boast the highest number of different species, with Southeast Asia only just behind. However, Asia probably contains distinct areas that hold a larger number of species than any similar-sized area in the Americas. Africa lags way behind for most organisms, although it is rich in primates; while Australasia misses out because of its relatively small forested area, although it contains a high proportion of endemics—species found nowhere else.

Much of the richest biodiversity is concentrated in a handful of countries called megadiversity countries. These all contain habitats in addition to tropical rain forests, such as dry forests, cool mountains, grasslands, and sometimes even deserts. However, in most of these megadiversity countries, their rain forests harbor the majority of their species.

Brazil is the country with the world's richest biodiversity in that it holds the highest number of plant and animal species within its borders. However, Brazil is a giant country, so if species-per-area is measured instead of just total number of species in the country, then Colombia and Indonesia compete for the top spot. Most of Brazil's biodiversity occurs in its rain forests, especially in the vast area of Amazonia. Brazil tops the world for the number of land-inhabiting vertebrates (over 3,000 species), freshwater fish (over 3,000 species, three times more than the highest total for any other country), amphibians (more than 500 species), and

IN FOCUS

Indonesia's Butterflies

Indonesia is home to as many as 121 species of swallowtails, which makes it a world leader. Even more astounding is that nearly half of them are found only in Indonesia.

Curimbata fish feed in the Paraguay River basin in the Mato Grosso region of Brazil. Amazonian rivers are home to an enormous variety of fish species.

flowering plants (some 55,000 species, nearly a quarter of the world total). Brazil's insect numbers can only be guessed at but probably exceed a million species.

Indonesia is quite different from Brazil in one important respect: rather than being a single vast country, it consists of hundreds of islands, both large and small, sprinkled across thousands of miles of tropical seas. It is by far the most biodiverse country in Asia and also has the highest proportion of its surface still covered with rain forests. These harbor almost 20,000 species of flowering plants, including the world's greatest variety of palms. Several important food plants originated in Indonesia, including sugarcane, citrus fruits, and black pepper. Indonesia also has a rich array of animals, coming out top in the world league for mammals (515 species, of which more than one-third are found nowhere else).

The highest biodiversity in Africa is found in the Congo River basin, where the giant Ituri Forest gives sanctuary to the bulk of the species. The Congo has the fourth highest total in the world for mammals (409 species) and comes second for freshwater fish. Several important endangered mammals live in the Congo, such as the okapi, mountain gorilla, and bonobo chimpanzee.

Madagascar's Biodiversity

Lying off the eastern coast of southern Africa, Madagascar is like a minicontinent, given the incredible length of the list of plants and animals that are unique to this vast and fragile island. Madagascar has been isolated for about 50 million years, allowing it to become a massive outdoor laboratory for the evolution of its own special species. Not only do 94 percent of its primates live only on Madagascar, but so do four out of the five primate families. Madagascar contains about half of all known species of chameleons (kuh-MEEL-yuhns), although not all of these are found in rain forests.

A Dangerous Time

Today biodiversity is in crisis, with many species on the way to extinction if the felling of tropical forests continues at the present rate. Only immediate worldwide action can save the tropical rain forests' rich biodiversity from disappearing forever.

Check these out:
- Amazonia ● Biomass ● Ecology
- Endangered Species ● Food Web
- Indonesia ● Madagascar ● Symbiosis

Bioluminescence

Bioluminescence is the production of light by living organisms. Many different kinds of marine creatures, especially those from the depths, produce light. In the rain forest, however, it is mainly insects and a few fungi (FUN-jie) that glow in the dark.

Although a variety of living things emit light, the chemistry of how they do it is similar in all of them. A chemical called luciferin reacts with oxygen from the air in the presence of another chemical, called luciferase, to produce the light. Unlike a lightbulb, which produces lots of heat as well as light and therefore wastes a lot of energy, bioluminescence is a cold light, expending only 5 percent of the energy as heat. It is perhaps a good thing that the light is cold, for it would be unfortunate for the insect if every time it wanted to glow it caught fire or had to eat that much more to supply the extra energy.

KEY FACTS

● **The light produced by insects is not just white but may also be green, red, or yellow.**

● **Organisms usually produce light to attract a mate or prey.**

● **Astronauts use luminescent fungi to check the purity of the air in their spaceship. If even small amounts of poisonous gases are present, the fungi stop making light.**

Luminous Insects

Most light-emitting insects are beetles. The ability is found in a number of families but is most common in the one that includes glowworms and fireflies. Special organs toward the tail end of the beetle's body produce light. Why?

A female glowworm, on Mount Kinabalu on Borneo, tries to attract males by producing light from the special organs at the end of her abdomen.

IN FOCUS

Lightning Bugs

Although fireflies are impressive in large numbers, the prize for light production for individual insects goes to the lightning bugs. These are luminescent click beetles. Some of the tropical American species reach as much as 3 in. (8 cm) in length, and they have been described as looking like flying flashlights.

Quite simply, it is to bring males and females together during the hours of darkness when they will be safely hidden from the birds and lizards that hunt them during the day. Each different kind of firefly has evolved its own pattern of flashing. Around 130 different species of fireflies exist today, though not all of them live in the world's rain forests. Some of the most spectacular examples live in Southeast Asia. In mangrove swamps lining the rivers and channels where the rain forests come down to the sea, thousands of the beetles may fly to a single tree. At first the fireflies flick their lights on and off every now and again. Eventually, however, they all get their timing right and blink on and off at the same time. For a moment the whole tree is lit up, then all is black again.

In the rain forests of New Zealand and Australia lives another type of insect that uses light, not a beetle but a kind of fly called a fungus gnat. It lives in forest caves, hollow trees, and under banks. Both the larvae and the adult females produce light. The larvae produce sticky threads that hang down from the roof where they live. Light from the larvae attracts small insects that get stuck on these threads. The larvae then crawl down the threads to feed on the trapped insects. To attract the males, the females emit light when they are fully formed but still inside the pupa. As the females hatch out, the males are waiting there to mate with them.

Luminescent Fungi

Although a number of kinds of rain forest fungi give out light, the purpose is unknown. Some kinds of fungi form glowing rings, while others occur in clumps. The thick overhead canopy of leaves makes the rain forest inky black at night, and the light from these fungi can be seen from a considerable distance.

A group of luminous fungi glow mysteriously on the forest floor of the Monteverde Cloud Forest Reserve in Costa Rica.

Check these out:
- Beetle ● Cave ● Fly ● Fungus
- ● Nocturnal Animal

Glossary

Aboriginal: the first of a kind known to exist in a particular country or area.

Afrikaans: the mother tongue of Afrikaners, South African settlers of Dutch descent.

Amazonia: the vast region in South America drained by the Amazon River.

Amphibian: a creature that may spend most of its life on land but must return to water to breed.

Antibiotic: a substance that prevents bacteria from multiplying.

Assimilate: to give up one's customs in order to live like people in the dominant culture.

Autonomy: a group of people that govern themselves; also, the right to self-govern.

Biodiversity: a measure of the numbers of species of living organisms found in a particular area.

Bromeliad: any of over one thousand plants of the pineapple family that have a crown of stiff, spiny leaves. Some bromeliads grow on the ground, but most of them are epiphytes.

Carnivore: a meat-eating animal or plant.

Carrion: dead animal remains.

Cellulose: a white chemical substance that forms the walls of plant cells and gives shape to the plant.

Dismember: to tear something to pieces.

Epiphyte: any plant that grows on another without taking any food from it. Most epiphytes grow on trees.

Grub: a larva with no legs. Grubs can be the larvae of bees, wasps, or many types of beetles.

Humus: the decomposed remains of plant material.

Hydroelectricity: electricity generated by the power of flowing water.

Indigenous: a plant or animal living in its native land.

Invertebrate: an animal that lacks a spinal column (backbone). Some invertebrates, such as insects, have a hard outer shell.

Irrigate: to supply extra water from streams, rivers, lakes, ponds, or reservoirs to agricultural land.

Larva (pl. larvae): a young insect that is markedly different from the adult and that has to pass through a pupal or chrysalis stage to reach maturity.

Marsupial: a mammal whose young are born very small and helpless after a brief pregnancy and that complete their development attached to their mother's teats, usually in a pouch called a marsupium.

Monsoon: a wind that results in a period of very heavy rains that fall on parts of India and Southeast Asia between April and September.

Nectar: the sweet liquid produced in flowers and sometimes elsewhere on plants. It attracts insects and other animals.

Omnivore: an animal that eats plants and animals.

Parasite: an organism (plant or animal) that lives off another living organism without benefiting that organism.

Pollen: the dustlike material produced by flowers. When carried to another flower by animals or the wind, it triggers the formation of seeds.

Polygamy: the practice of a person being married to more than one other person at a time.

Predator: any animal that kills other animals for food.

Prehensile: a limb that is able to grasp like a hand.

Primate: an animal of the family of apes and monkeys, including humans.

Rabies: a disease caused by a virus that affects the nervous system and unless treated at an early stage is always fatal.

Scavenger: a creature that feeds mainly on the remains of dead plants or animals.

Secondary rain forest: new growth of plants and trees that fills a small area of forest that had been cleared.

Silt: soil washed off the land and down rivers in areas of heavy rainfall.

Slash-and-burn: a form of agriculture that involves cutting down all the trees in a given area and then burning whatever is left. The land is then used for farming, benefiting in the short-term from the nutrients released by the burned vegetation.

Social insect: an insect species that lives in a colony containing numerous individuals with different tasks. All the insects work for the good of the whole community.

Solitary insect: an insect species where individuals do not group up to form complex societies.

Stamen: the part of a flower that produces pollen.

Synchronize: to happen or make happen at exactly the same time.

Tributary: a small stream or river which flows into a larger stream or river.

Vegetarian: an animal that eats only plant food; also known as a herbivore.

Index